Modern Art Stitching

Debra Valencia

LEISURE ARTS, INC. • Maumelle, Arkansas

TABLE OF CONTENTS

INTRODUCTION

I absolutely love needle arts! I look forward to starting each day with a couple of hours of stitching. It is so relaxing and satisfying to see my designs come to life in this medium. The Cross Stitched elements provide colored shapes with a soft feel of the fabric showing through. Feel free to make your own variations of these designs by simplifying or adding more details. Try stitching these patterns onto other projects too. A design for a pillow can be put on a tote bag. A pattern for a tea towel can become a tablet case.

DEBRA VALENCIA

ABOUT THE AUTHOR

Debra Valencia, a visionary artist, designer and entrepreneur with a passion for world travel, artisan traditions, pop art, fashion and everything vintage has branded a modern look uniquely her own. Her designs take a fresh approach to creatively blending florals, paisleys, geometric and decorative motifs with a distinctive sense of style. Her bright colors and bold elements can be described as chic and sassy. Debra's artwork is licensed to dozens of manufacturers in the gift, stationery, textiles, home décor, fashion accessories and beauty industries with 1000s of products in a variety of retailers.

Debra graduated with honors with a BFA from the University of the Arts in Philadelphia. She worked as a graphic designer and creative director for several companies in the early years of her career. She has won numerous professional design awards such as AIGA's 50 Best Books of the Year. Her work has been featured in dozens of publications including Time, Communication Arts, Print, Abitare, Elle Décor, Greetings Etc., Giftware News and License Global! to name a few.

As an art educator for over 15 years, Debra has served as a part-time faculty member at Otis College of Art & Design in Los Angeles and at Art Center College of Design in Pasadena. Courses taught include Licensing Your Art for Royalties, Surface Design, Graphic Design, Typography, Embroidery and more. Debra has lectured at major institutions including Cal Poly Tech, Harvard University, University of Wisconsin Madison and FIDM, and at national conferences such as AIGA (American Institute of Graphic Arts), SEGD (Society of Experiential Graphic Designers) and AFCI (Association for Creative Industries). She has served as a judge of her peers in numerous national design competitions.

Debra is an experienced seamstress and has been enjoying needle arts and other crafts since childhood. Her designs have been produced as quilting fabric collections for Fabric Editions, South Sea Imports, Wilmington Prints and David Textiles resulting in thousands of yards sold since 2009. She is the co-author of Sewing Pretty Bags and the author of four designer coloring books, three embroidery books, and two Diamond Dotz® books.

Debra lives in Los Angeles, California in a Cliff May mid-century modern home built in 1953 surrounded by vintage collectibles, iconic furniture by Charles Eames and George Nelson and original artwork by her artist friends. Debra's son, Westin Walker, is an illustrator, graphic designer and fine artist with a BFA from California College of Art. He collaborates on professional projects with his mother and contributed the charts for this book.

Visit my website, www.debravalencia.com where you will find craft patterns, project ideas, and my online shops. Please follow me on Facebook and Instagram for news and updates. I would love to hear from you and see your creations. Feel free to post questions, comments and photos to share with other fans on social media.

Author Website and Contacts:
www.debravalencia.com
Facebook: www.facebook.com/debravalenciadesigns
Instragram: @debravalencia

ACKNOWLEDGEMENTS

My publisher, Tona Jolly and the team at Leisure Arts have been so patient and generous with their support, and their warm reception to my project ideas and designs. I appreciate this opportunity to do what I love as my job: draw, design, teach and make. Thank you to my son, Westin, for his expert computer work and attention to detail on the charts.

DEDICATION

To JA for your love, patience and support.

MOD PINCUSHION

This simple pincushion is an easy beginner project to make for yourself. It also makes a functional but fun gift. I've even included three bonus charts to give you some additional choices for more creative cushions.

Finished Size: Approx. 3" x 3" inserted in a 2¾" diameter x 1" high pincushion

STITCH GUIDE

- All Cross Stitches stitched over one square using 3 strands of floss.

SHOPPING LIST

- ☐ Clover brand #4121 Create-a-Pincushion or similar
- ☐ 6" x 6" piece of black 14 count Aida cloth
- ☐ Small handful of polyester fiberfill
- ☐ Fabric marking pencil, white
- ☐ Embroidery hoop (optional)
- ☐ Tapestry needle, size 22 to 28
- ☐ 1 skein each of DMC® 6-strand embroidery floss
  - White
  - Charcoal gray: 535

INSTRUCTIONS

Charts for this design and 3 bonus designs are found on pages 26 - 27.

1. Locate the center of the fabric by folding the fabric in half, side to side, and again top to bottom; mark this point with a straight pin.
2. Starting in the center and counting squares of the Aida cloth, Cross Stitch the design.
3. If you have used a marking pencil to define stitching areas, hold the project under running tap water. The markings will disappear in seconds. Place the piece right side down on a thick white towel. Press the piece dry from the wrong side with an iron temperature suitable for the type of fabric used.
4. Fill the base of the pincushion with polyester fiberfill, packing in as much as possible for a dense filling.
5. Centering the design, place the silicone retainer ring over the stitched piece and base.
6. Trim excess fabric around the base of the pincushion.
7. Place the collar over the base.

GEO JEWELRY SETS

Included here and on pages 10-11 are two design options, Rainbow Square and Triple Cross. The design and color variations are endless for these tiny wearable art pieces. Make them for yourself or as gifts for friends and family.

Pendant

Rainbow Square Finished Size: ⅞" x ⅞" inserted in a 1⅛" diameter pendant

Triple Cross Finished Size: 1" x 1" inserted in a 1⅛" diameter pendant

Bracelet

Rainbow Square Finished Size: 5⁄16" x 5¾" inserted in a ½" wide x 6¾" long bangle bracelet

Triple Cross Finished Size: 5⁄16" x 5¾" inserted in a ½" wide x 6¾" long bangle bracelet

STITCH GUIDE

• All Cross Stitches stitched over one square using 2 strands of floss.

SHOPPING LIST

- ☐ Cutesy Crafts embroidery necklace frame kit, large, silver or gold plated, and 14" to 18" chain as desired
- ☐ Bangle bracelet blank with channel, silver or gold plated, ½" wide x 6¾" long
- ☐ 3" x 3" piece of black 14 count Aida cloth for pendant
- ☐ 3" x 9" piece of black 14 count Aida cloth for bracelet
- ☐ Fabric marking pencil, white
- ☐ Tapestry needle, size 22 to 28
- ☐ Black sewing thread, cotton or polyester
- ☐ White liquid glue
- ☐ Hot glue gun

Rainbow Square Pendant Necklace and Bangle Bracelet

☐ 1 skein each of DMC® 6-strand embroidery floss

- Yellow: 728
- Orange: 720
- Red: 321
- Fuchsia: 718
- Purple: 333

Triple Cross Pendant Necklace and Bangle Bracelet

☐ 1 skein each of DMC® 6-strand embroidery floss

- Red: 321
- Gray: 535
- White

GEO JEWELRY SETS *(CONTINUED)*

INSTRUCTIONS

Charts are found on pages 28 - 29.

Pendant

1. Locate the center of the fabric by folding the fabric in half, side to side, and again top to bottom; mark this point with a straight pin.
2. Starting in the center and counting squares of the Aida cloth, Cross Stitch the design.
3. If you have used a marking pencil to define stitching areas, hold the project under running tap water. The markings will disappear in seconds. Place the piece right side down on a thick white towel. Press the piece dry from the wrong side with an iron temperature suitable for the type of fabric used.
4. Place the stitched piece face down. Center the insert that came with the pendant over the stitched area and use a marking pencil to draw around the insert.
5. Using the black sewing thread and leaving about 3" tails on each end, stitch long running stitches about ⅛" outside the drawn line.
6. Trim excess fabric outside the running stitches as needed, cutting the fabric into a circle.
7. Pulling the threads as tight as possible and adjusting the position of the stitching to assure it is centered, tie the two tails together to gather the fabric around the insert; trim off excess thread. Press all the excess fabric to flatten.
8. Using a hot glue gun, apply a bead of glue about the size of a pea to the back of the insert. Place into pendant frame; press firmly in place until glue cools.

Bracelet

1. Locate the center of the fabric by folding the fabric in half, side to side, and again top to bottom; mark this point with a straight pin.
2. Starting in the center and counting squares of the Aida cloth, Cross Stitch the design.
3. If you have used a marking pencil to define stitching areas, hold the project under running tap water. The markings will disappear in seconds. Place the piece right side down on a thick white towel. Press the piece dry from the wrong side with an iron temperature suitable for the type of fabric used.
4. Centering the design, trim the fabric to approx. ½" wide x 6¾" long to fit inside channel of bracelet.
5. Using the white liquid glue, apply a light coat of glue on entire back side of fabric.
6. Carefully place into channel and adjust placement as needed; press firmly in place until glue dries.

GEO TRINKET BOX

The trinket box has many uses from a desk organizer for paper clips, a coin saver or a small jewelry box for earrings or rings. Consider painting or staining the wooden box prior to stitching.

Finished Size: 3" x 3" stitched on a 3⅞" wide x 3⅞" long x 2¾" high trinket box

STITCH GUIDE

- All Cross Stitches stitched over one square using 1 strand of pearl cotton.

SHOPPING LIST

Project shown is stitch with Eleganza brand #8 Pearl Cotton but DMC® #8 Pearl Cotton may be substituted.

- ☐ Dimensions™ DIY stitchable wood trinket box or similar, 3⅞" wide x 3⅞" long x 2¾" high, 10 stitches per inch
- ☐ 1 ball each of Eleganza™ #8 Pearl Cotton or DMC® #8 Pearl Cotton

Color	*Eleganza*	*DMC®*
• Olive green	146	3346
• Straw yellow	126	744
• Aqua green	810	943
• Slate blue	722	519
• Baby blue	716	809
• Coral	922	352
• Orange yellow	206	972
• Purple	506	209

- ☐ Tapestry needle, size 18
- ☐ White liquid glue (optional)
- ☐ Felt (optional)

INSTRUCTIONS

Chart is found on page 30.

1. Starting in the upper left corner and counting predrilled holes in the box, Cross Stitch the design.
2. **Optional:** Cut a piece of felt for inside cover of lid; secure in place with glue.

CHEVRON EYEGLASS CASE

This sleek but colorful design for your eyeglasses is fun and fashionable. Shown here in a full spectrum of colors, this design can be made to be more subtle with just a two color scheme.

Finished Size: ***Small*** – 2½" x 7⅛" finished to 3¼" wide x 7⅝" long
Large – 2½" x 7⅛" finished to 3¾" wide x 7⅝" long

STITCH GUIDE

- All Cross Stitches stitched over one square using 2 strands of floss.

SHOPPING LIST

- ☐ 10" x 10" piece of black 14 count Aida cloth
- ☐ Fabric marking pencil, white
- ☐ Tapestry needle, size 22 to 28
- ☐ Embroidery hoop (optional)
- ☐ 1 skein each of DMC® 6-strand embroidery floss
  - Fuchsia: 3607
  - Light pink: 776
  - Light coral: 3825
  - Orange: 721
  - Yellow: 728
  - Cream: 745
  - Lime green: 3819
  - Green: 704
  - Teal: 3812
  - Light aqua: 964
  - Lavender: 554
  - Purple: 3746
  - Black: 310

INSTRUCTIONS

Chart is found on page 31.

1. Beginning 1" from top edge and left edge and counting squares of the Aida cloth, Cross stitch the design.
2. If you have used a marking pencil to define stitching areas, hold the project under running tap water. The markings will disappear in seconds. Place the piece right side down on a thick white towel. Press the piece dry from the wrong side with an iron temperature suitable for the type of fabric used.
3. Leaving 4 fabric squares beyond stitched area, trim top and bottom edges all the way across fabric.
4. Trim left side of fabric, leaving 6 fabric squares for small eyeglass case or 10 squares for large eyeglass case.
5. Fold right side of case to the back, leaving 6 fabric squares showing on the right side for small eyeglass case or 10 squares showing on the right side for large eyeglass case; press to crease.
6. Trim excess fabric on back even with left edge of eyeglass case.
7. Using 6 strands of black floss, unfold and stitch along the top edge with a Blanket Stitch.
8. Refold and stitch the side and bottom edges together with a Blanket Stitch.

CONTEMPO COASTER SET

Playful geometric shapes make unique compositions for each coaster. Try out a new color scheme to match your taste or home décor scheme.

Finished Size: 4" x 4" stitched on a 4⅛" x 4⅛" square of 14 mesh perforated plastic canvas

STITCH GUIDE

- All Half Cross Stitches stitched over one square using 1 strand of pearl cotton.

SHOPPING LIST

- ☐ 8½" x 11" sheet of 14 mesh perforated plastic canvas
- ☐ X-Acto® knife or utility knife
- ☐ Metal ruler or cutting edge
- ☐ Tapestry needle, size 18
- ☐ 1 skein each of DMC® #5 Pearl Cotton
    - Orange: 351
    - Yellow: 725
    - Green: 943
    - Slate blue: 807
    - Grey: 03
    - Purple: 208
- ☐ Felt (optional)
- ☐ White liquid glue (optional)
- ☐ Self-stick clear rubber bumpers or pads (optional)

INSTRUCTIONS

Charts are found on pages 32 - 33.

1. Using the X-Acto knife or utility knife with metal ruler or cutting edge, cut 4 pieces of plastic canvas 4⅛" x 4⅛". There should be 56 stitches in each direction.
2. When working with plastic canvas which is a rigid material, it is not necessary to start in the center. Starting in the upper left corner and counting holes in the plastic canvas, use Half Cross Stitches to complete one coaster. Stitch the additional three coasters in the same manner.
3. Optional protection on bottom:

   a. Cut 4" x 4" pieces of felt for bottom of coasters. Secure with small dabs of glue.

   b. Apply self-stick clear rubber bumpers or pads which are sold for glass table tops, cabinet doors and other uses. The bumpers will raise the coaster so that it is not in direct contact with the table surface.

BAUHAUS ART GALLERY

Make your own miniature art gallery with these Bauhaus inspired modern compositions. Shown here in classic primary colors, these designs would also look good in earth tones or bright colors alike.

Finished Size: 4 3/8" x 6 1/4" inserted in a 5" x 7" frame

STITCH GUIDE

• All Backstitch stitched over two squares using 6 strands of floss.

SHOPPING LIST

- ☐ Four 8" x 10" pieces of oatmeal 14 count Aida cloth
- ☐ Fabric marking pen, blue, water-soluble
- ☐ Tapestry needle, size 22 to 28
- ☐ Embroidery hoop (optional)
- ☐ 2 skeins each of DMC® 6-strand embroidery floss
  - Red: 321
  - Yellow: 728
  - Blue: 798
  - Orange: 721
  - Green: 700
  - Black: 310
- ☐ Four standard picture frames with 5" x 7" openings, your choice of color and style

INSTRUCTIONS

Charts are found on pages 34 - 35.

1. Locate the center of the fabric by folding the fabric in half, side to side, and again top to bottom; mark this point with a straight pin.
2. Starting in the center and counting squares of the Aida cloth, Backstitch the design.
3. If you have used a marking pen or pencil to define stitching areas, hold the project under running tap water. The markings will disappear in seconds. Place the piece right side down on a thick white towel. Press the piece dry from the wrong side with an iron temperature suitable for the type of fabric used.
4. Disassemble the frames and clean glass.
5. Centering the stitched piece, trim the fabric to 5" x 7" using the picture frame glass as a guide.
6. Center the stitched pieces on the glass facing down and sandwiched between glass and back board. Assemble the frames.

GRAPHIC HOOP TRIAD

You can make just one of these designs or make all three for a modern triad display.

Finished Sizes:

Large Hoop: 5¾" x 5¾" inserted in a 7" diameter hoop

Medium Hoop: 4" x 3½" inserted in a 5" diameter hoop

Small Hoop: 2⅜" x 2⅜" inserted in a 4" diameter hoop

STITCH GUIDE

- All Half Cross Stitches stitched over one square using 3 strands of floss.
- All Backstitches stitched over two squares using 3 strands of floss.

SHOPPING LIST

- ☐ One 10" x 10" piece, one 8" x 8" piece, and one 7" x 7" piece of gray 14 count Aida cloth
- ☐ Three bamboo hoops, 7" diameter, 5" diameter, and 4" diameter
- ☐ Fabric marking pen, blue, water-soluble
- ☐ Tapestry needle, size 22 to 28
- ☐ Embroidery hoop (optional)
- ☐ 1 skein each of DMC® 6-strand embroidery floss
  - Yellow: 728
  - Pink: 3706
  - Coral: 3853
  - Lavender: 210
  - Slate blue: 597
  - Olive green: 3347
  - Lime green: 472
  - Gray: 415
  - Aqua: 993
- ☐ **Optional:** Gray watercolor paint or translucent marker

INSTRUCTIONS

Charts are found on pages 36 - 37.

1. Locate the center of the fabric by folding the fabric in half, side to side, and again top to bottom; mark this point with a straight pin.
2. Starting in the center and counting squares of the Aida cloth, stitch Half Cross Stitches and Backstitches to complete the designs.
3. If you have used a marking pen to define stitching areas, hold the project under running tap water. The markings will disappear in seconds. Place the piece right side down on a thick white towel. Press the piece dry from the wrong side with an iron temperature suitable for the type of fabric used.
4. **Optional:** Tint the bamboo hoops with watercolor paint or a translucent marker; allow to thoroughly dry.
5. Refer to **Using Hoops for Display**, page 47, for assembly instructions.

spice cookies

MCM TEA TOWEL SET

MCM, also known as Mid-Century Modern, is the period of modern design from 1945 to 1965. This modernist movement is still very popular today and can be described as chic and elegant. This tea towel set will fit right into that look.

Finished Size: 2¼" x 13¼" stitched on a 15" wide x 25" long tea towel

STITCH GUIDE

• All Cross Stitches stitched over two fabric threads using 2 strands of floss.

SHOPPING LIST

- ☐ Two DMC® Charles Craft® French Market linen-look tea towels, natural light, 40 count, 15" wide x 25" long, or similar
- ☐ Fabric marking pen, blue, water-soluble
- ☐ Tapestry needle, size 22 to 28
- ☐ Embroidery hoop (optional)
- ☐ 1 skein each of DMC® 6-strand embroidery floss
  - Orange: 721
  - Ochre yellow: 3852
  - Olive green: 470
  - Aqua: 564

INSTRUCTIONS

Charts are found on pages 38 - 39.

1. Using the marking pen, draw a line 6" from the long right edge of the towel.
2. Beginning at bottom of towel and stitching over 2 fabric threads, Cross Stitch 2 vertical rows using DMC® 564 along the drawn line for approx. 2".
3. Referring to charts, Cross Stitch a square or rectangle in desired floss colors. Cross Stitch 2 vertical rows using DMC® 564 along the drawn line for approx. 1".
4. Repeat in this manner for desired number of squares and/or rectangles. If desired, continue the long vertical line of stitches all the way to the other end of the towel.
5. If you have used a marking pen or pencil to define stitching areas, hold the project under running tap water. The markings will disappear in seconds. Place the towel right side down on a thick white towel. Press the towel dry from the wrong side with an iron temperature suitable for the type of fabric used.

RETRO PILLOW DUO

Ready-made pillow covers are available in many colors. Shop for linen or linen-look fabrics with an even weave. Change the color scheme to coordinate with your own home décor. These are easy projects to make resulting in elegant home accents for the living room, den or bedroom.

Finished Size:
Square pillow: 10½" x 10½" stitched on a 16" x 16" pillow cover
Lumbar pillow: 15⅞" x 10⅛" stitched on a 20" x 12" pillow cover

STITCH GUIDE

- All Backstitch stitched over two fabric threads using 6 strands of floss.

SHOPPING LIST

- ☐ One 16" x 16" black ready-made square pillow cover, even weave linen or similar, 10 count
- ☐ One 12" x 20" black ready-made lumbar pillow cover, even weave linen or similar, 10 count
- ☐ One 16" x 16" and one 12" x 20" ready-made pillow insert
- ☐ Fabric marking pencil, whites
- ☐ Tapestry needle, size 18
- ☐ Embroidery hoop (optional)
- ☐ 2 skeins each of DMC® 6-strand embroidery floss (except where otherwise indicated)
  - Ecru
  - Lime green: 166 (3 skeins)
  - Aqua: 992
  - Gray: 414

INSTRUCTIONS

Charts are found on pages 40 - 43.

1. Locate the center of the pillow cover by folding the cover in half, side to side, and again top to bottom; mark this point with a straight pin.
2. Starting in the center and counting fabric threads of the pillow cover, Backstitch the design.
3. If you have used a marking pencil to define stitching areas, hold the project under running tap water. The markings will disappear in seconds. Place the cover right side down on a thick white towel. Press the cover dry from the wrong side with an iron temperature suitable for the type of fabric used.
4. Insert standard pillow inserts into each cover.

MOD PINCUSHION

Finished Size: Approx. 3" x 3" inserted in a 2¾" diameter x 1" high pincushion

STITCH GUIDE

• All Cross Stitches stitched over one square using 3 strands of floss.

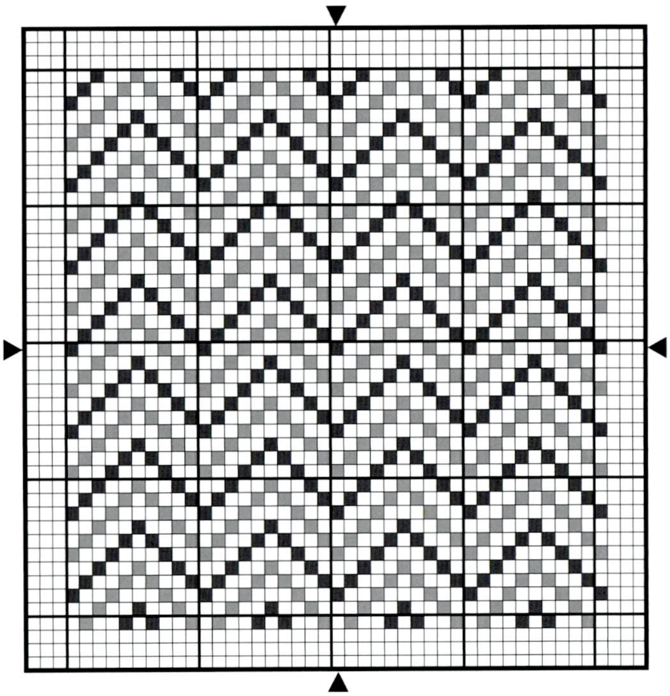

PINCUSHION 1

41 squares x 41 squares

PINCUSHION 2

41 squares x 41 squares

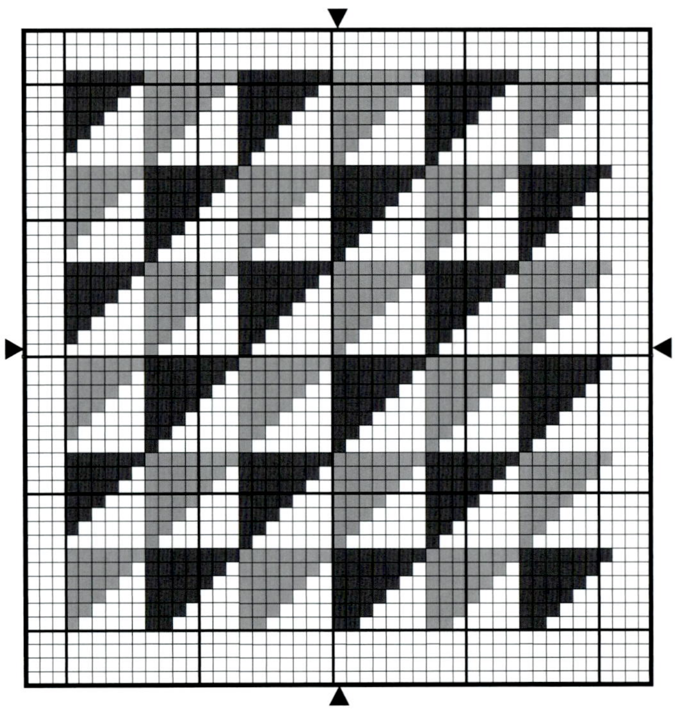

DMC Colors For Charts

X	DMC
● (dark)	535
● (gray)	White

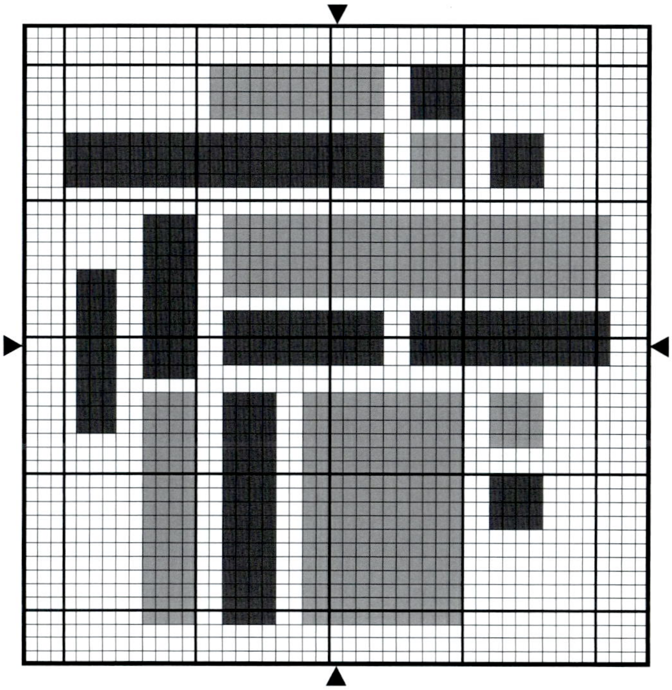

PINCUSHION 3

41 squares x 41 squares

PINCUSHION 4

41 squares x 41 squares

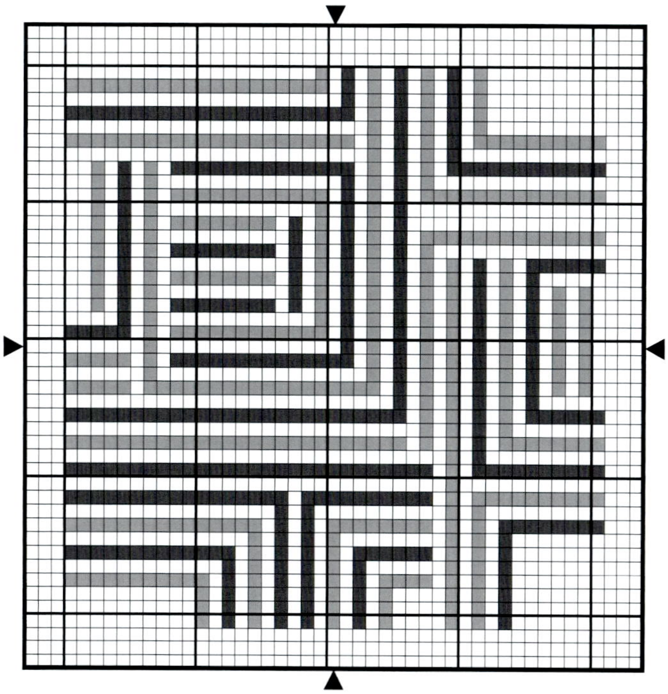

GEO JEWELRY SETS

STITCH GUIDE

• All Cross Stitches stitched over one square using 2 strands of floss.

Pendant

Triple Cross Finished Size: 1" x 1" inserted in a 1⅛" diameter pendant

Bracelet

Triple Cross Finished Size: 5⁄16" x 5¾" inserted in a ½" wide x 6¾" long bangle bracelet

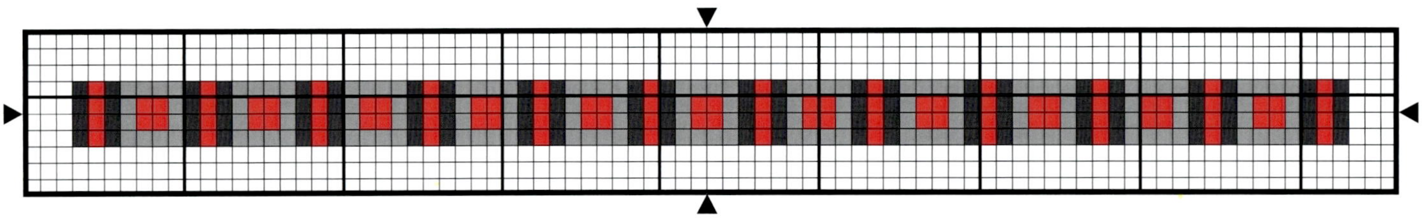

BRACELET

Triple Cross
80 squares x 4 squares

DMC Colors For Charts

X	DMC
● (red)	321
● (dark gray)	535
● (blue)	White

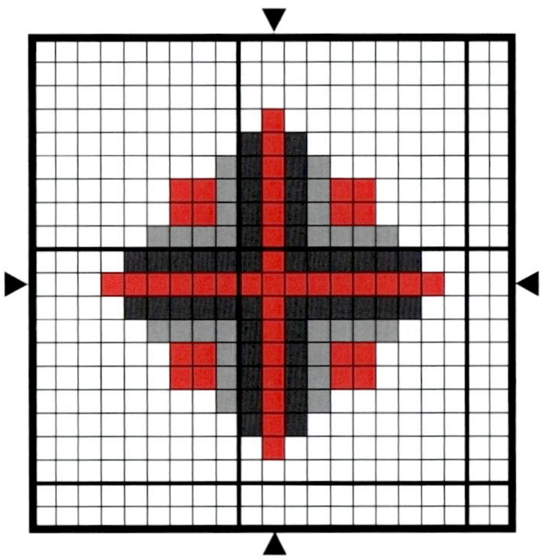

PENDANT

15 squares x 15 squares

Pendant

Rainbow Square Finished Size: ⅞" x ⅞" inserted in a 1⅛" diameter pendant

Bracelet

Rainbow Square Finished Size: 5/16" x 5¾" inserted in a ½" wide x 6¾" long bangle bracelet

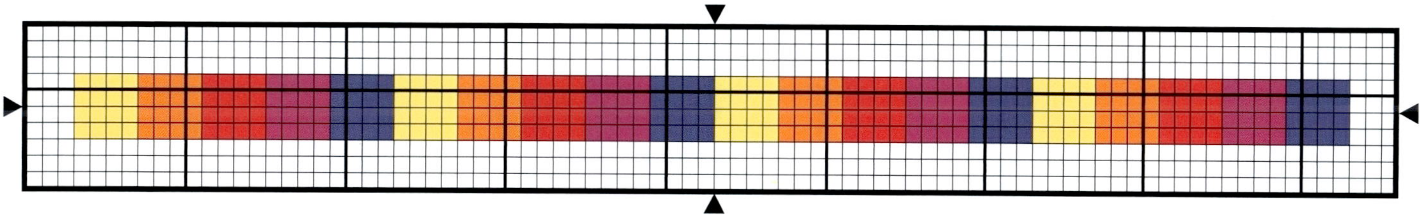

BRACELET

Rainbow Square
80 squares x 4 squares

DMC Colors For Charts

X	DMC
	728
	720
	321
	718
	333

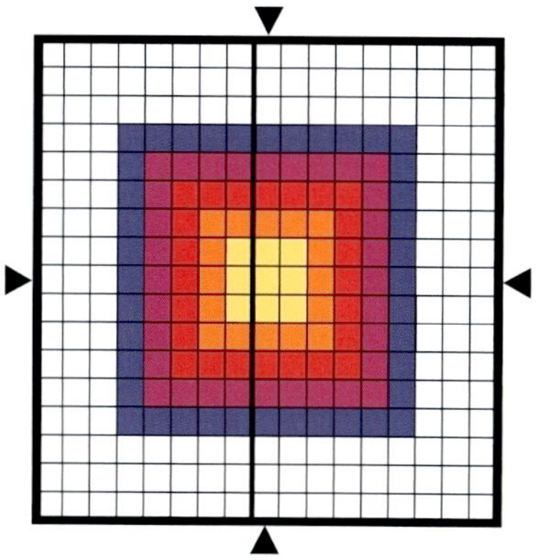

PENDANT

11 squares x 11 squares

GEO TRINKET BOX

Finished Size: 3" x 3" stitched on a 3⅞" wide x 3⅞" long x 2¾" high trinket box

STITCH GUIDE

- All Cross Stitches stitched over one square using 1 strand of pearl cotton.

TRINKET BOX

31 squares x 31 squares

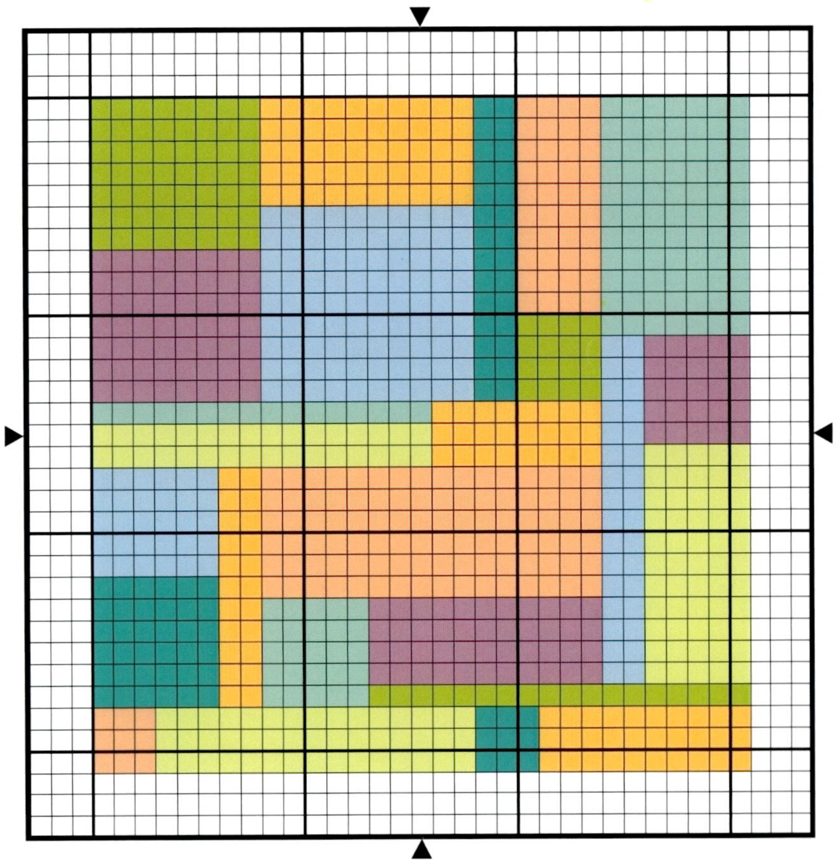

DMC Colors For Charts

X	Eleganza	DMC
	146	3346
	126	744
	810	943
	722	519
	716	809
	922	352
	206	972
	506	209

CHEVRON EYEGLASS CASE

Finished Size: ***Small*** – 2½" x 7⅛" finished to 3¼" wide x 7⅝" long

Large – 2½" x 7⅛" finished to 3¾" wide x 7⅝" long

STITCH GUIDE

- All Cross Stitches stitched over one square using 2 strands of floss.

EYEGLASS CASE

35 squares x 99 squares

DMC Colors For Charts

X	DMC
	3607
	776
	3825
	721
	728
	745
	3819
	704
	3812
	964
	554
	3746

CONTEMPO COASTER SET

Finished Size: 4" x 4" stitched on a 4⅛" x 4⅛" square of 14 mesh perforated plastic canvas

STITCH GUIDE

- All Half Cross Stitches stitched over one square using 1 strand of pearl cotton.

ALL COASTERS

56 squares x 56 squares

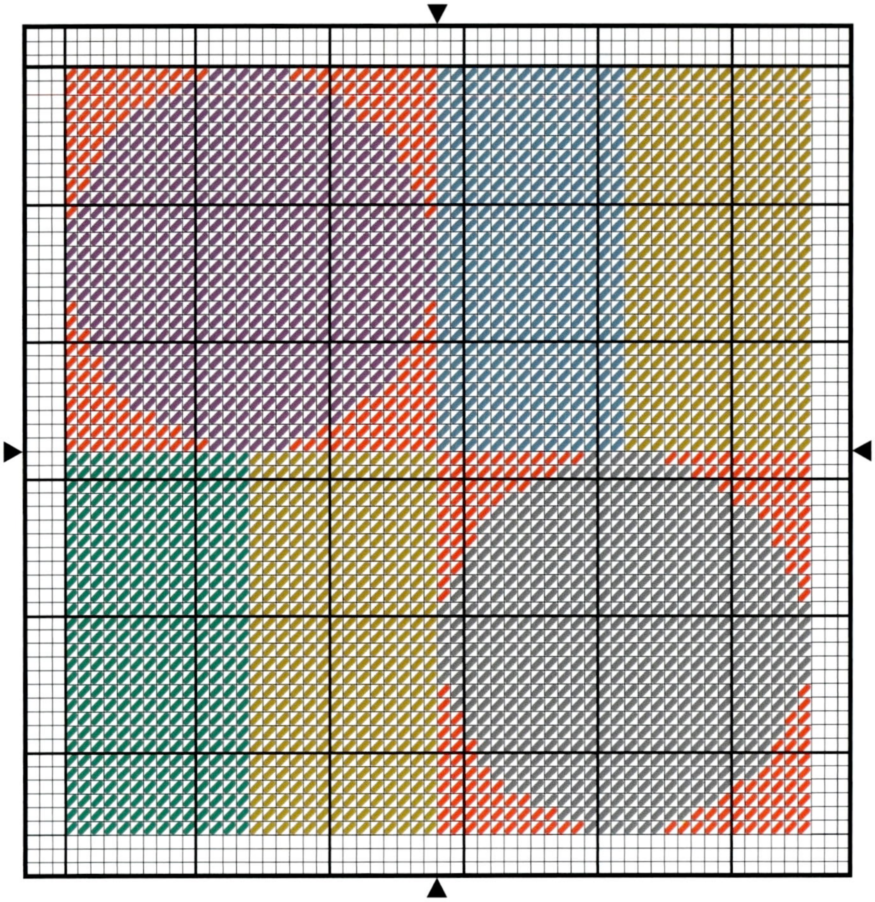

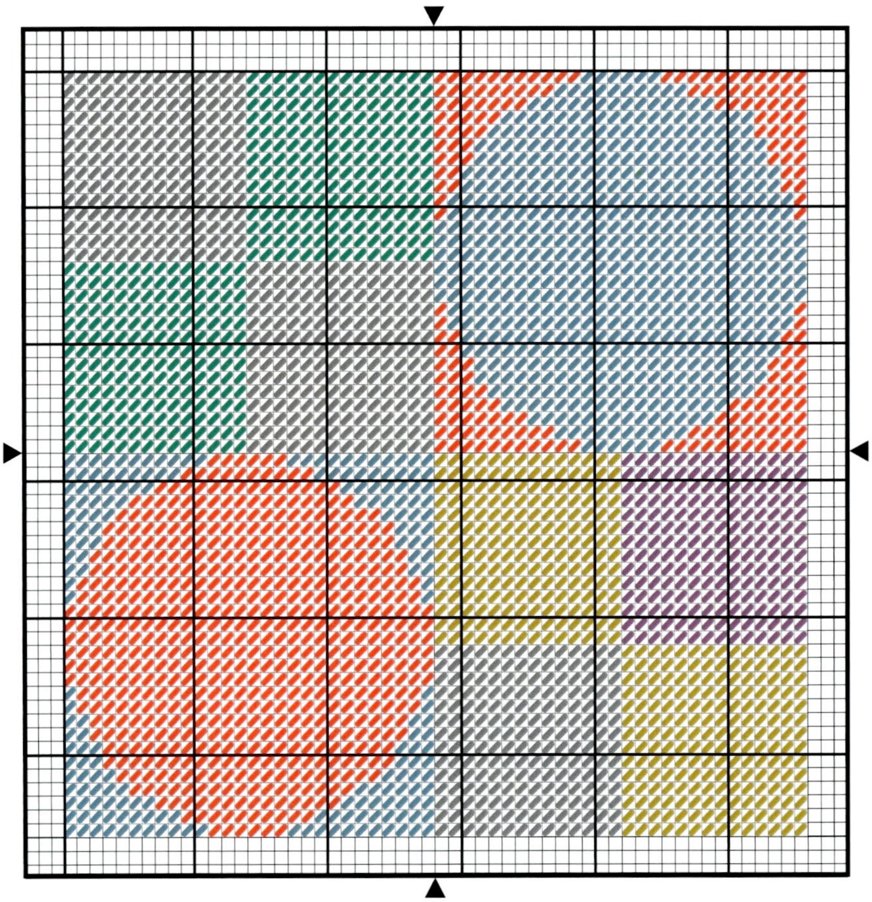

DMC Colors For Charts

X	DMC
(orange-red)	351
(gold)	725
(green)	943
(blue)	807
(gray)	03
(purple)	208

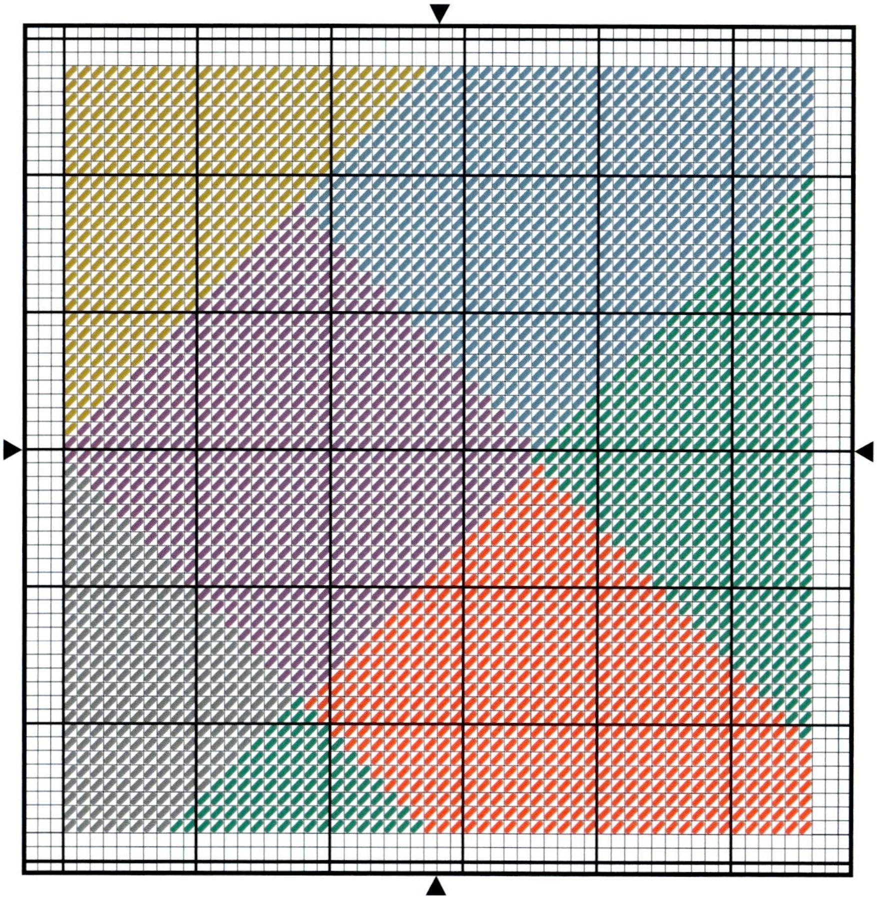

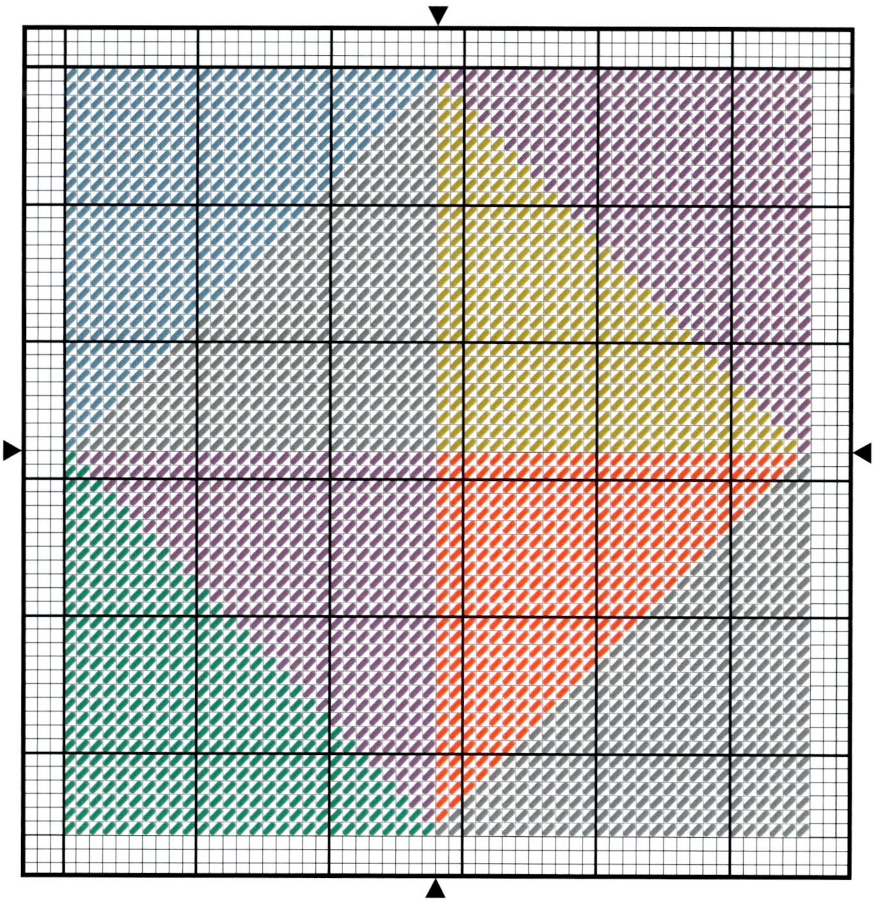

BAUHAUS ART GALLERY

Finished Size: 4 3/8" x 6 1/4" inserted in a 5" x 7" frame

STITCH GUIDE

- All Backstitch stitched over two squares using 6 strands of floss.

BAUHAUS 1

56 squares x 84 squares

BAUHAUS 2

60 squares x 86 squares

BAUHAUS 3

58 squares x 86 squares

BAUHAUS 4

59 squares x 84 squares

DMC Colors For Charts

X	DMC
	321
	728
	798
	721
	700
	310

1

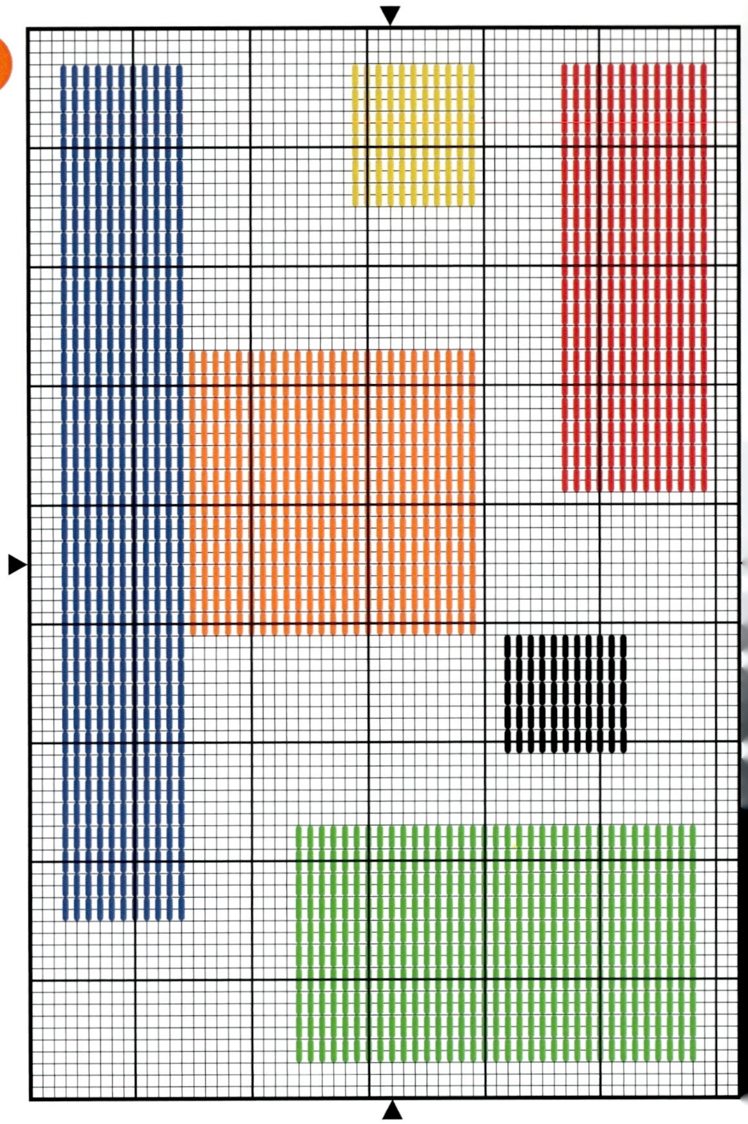

2

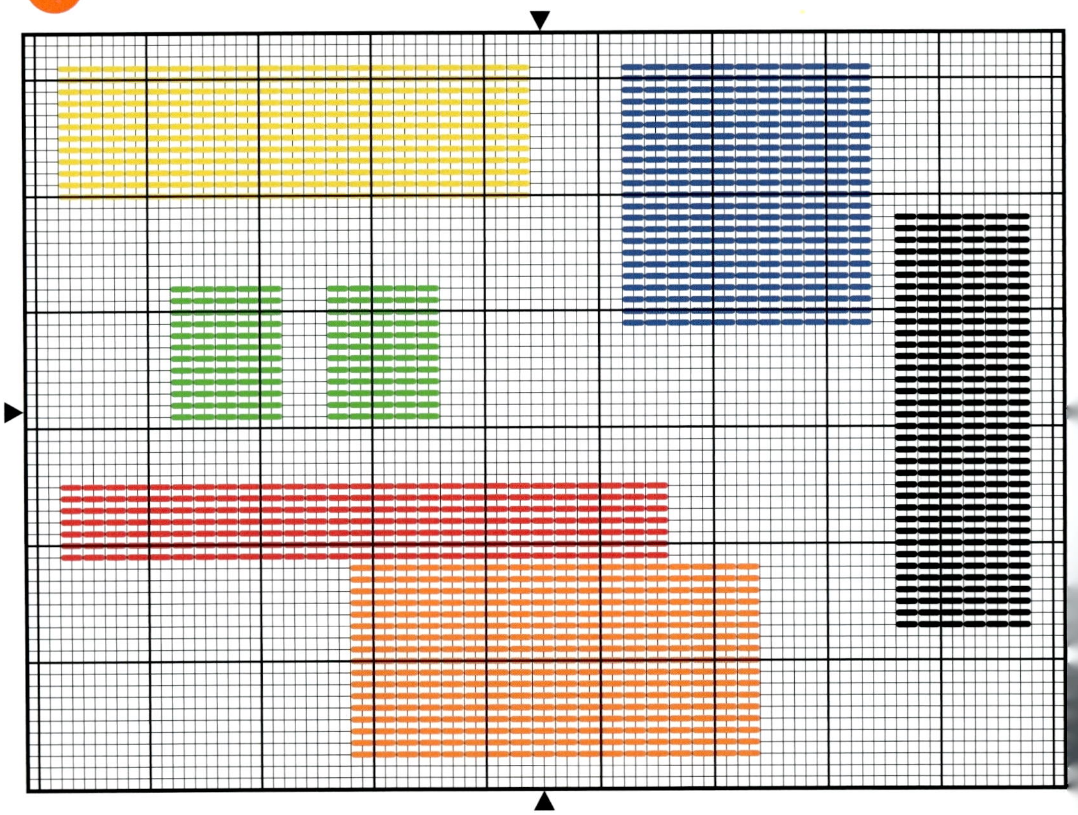

3

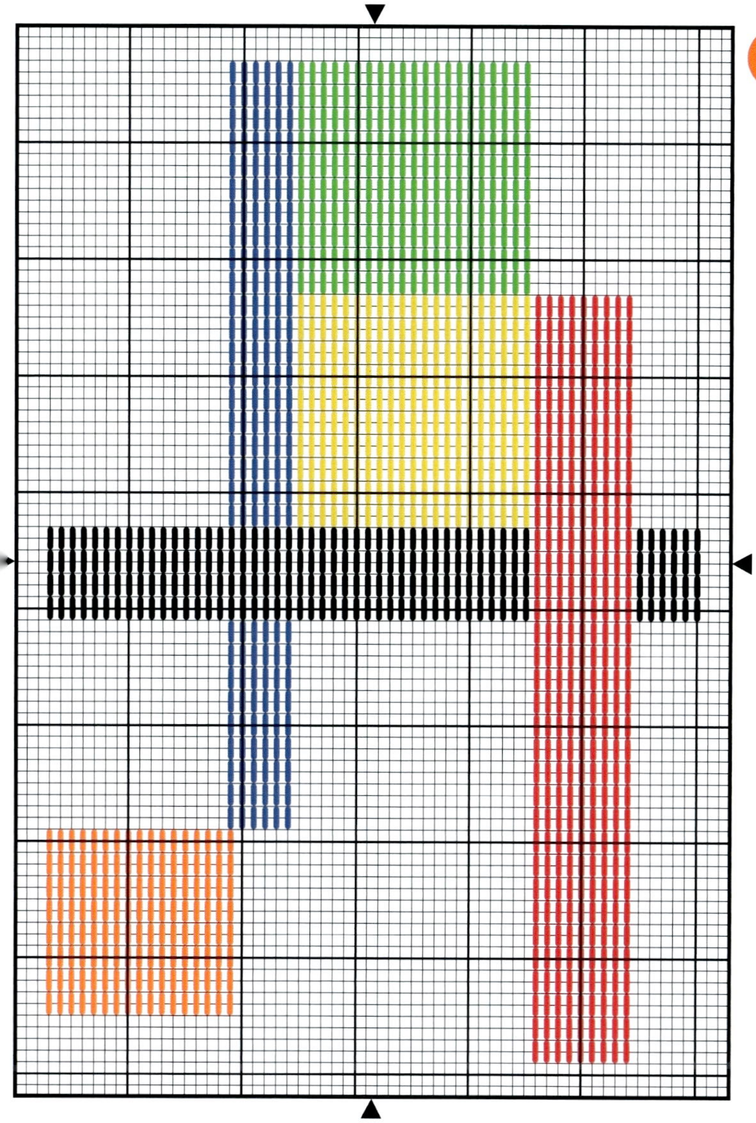

4

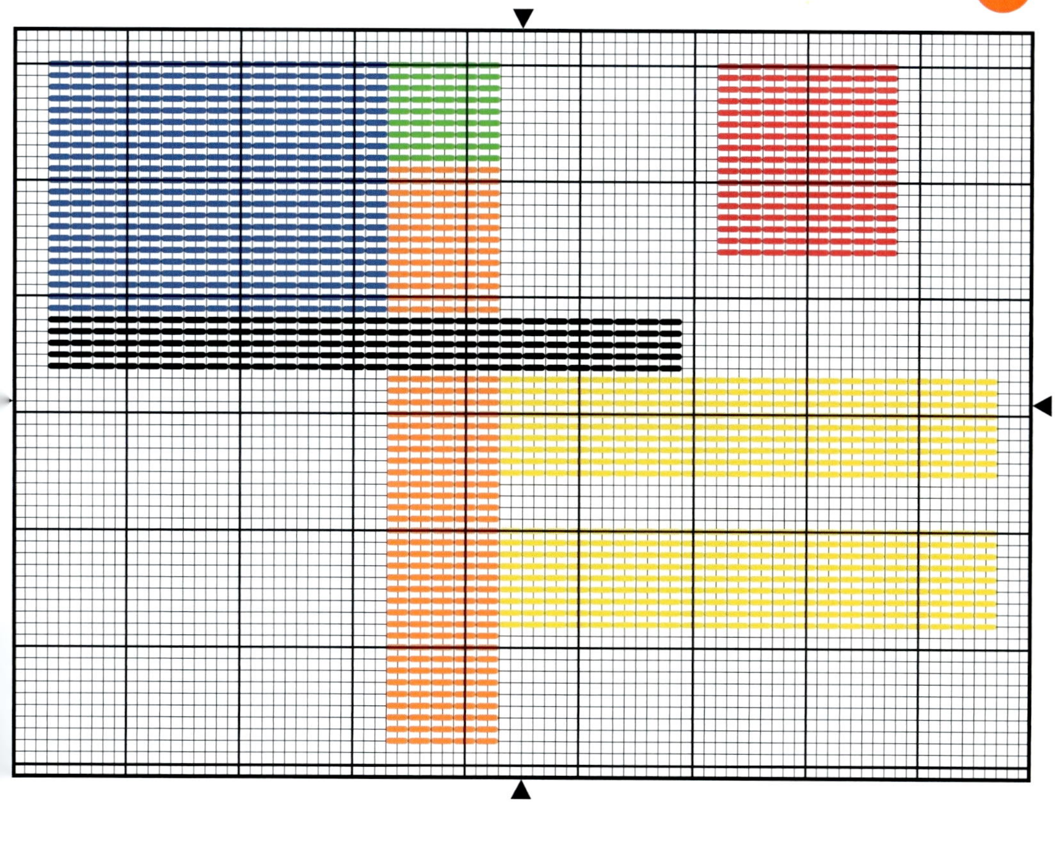

GRAPHIC HOOP TRIAD

Finished Sizes:

Large Hoop: 5¾" x 5¾" inserted in a 7" diameter hoop

Medium Hoop: 4" x 3½" inserted in a 5" diameter hoop

Small Hoop: 2⅜" x 2⅜" inserted in a 4" diameter hoop

STITCH GUIDE

- All Half Cross Stitches stitched over one square using 3 strands of floss.
- All Backstitches stitched over two squares using 3 strands of floss.

HOOP 1

56 squares x 48 squares

HOOP 2

80 squares x 80 squares

HOOP 3

33 squares x 33 squares

1

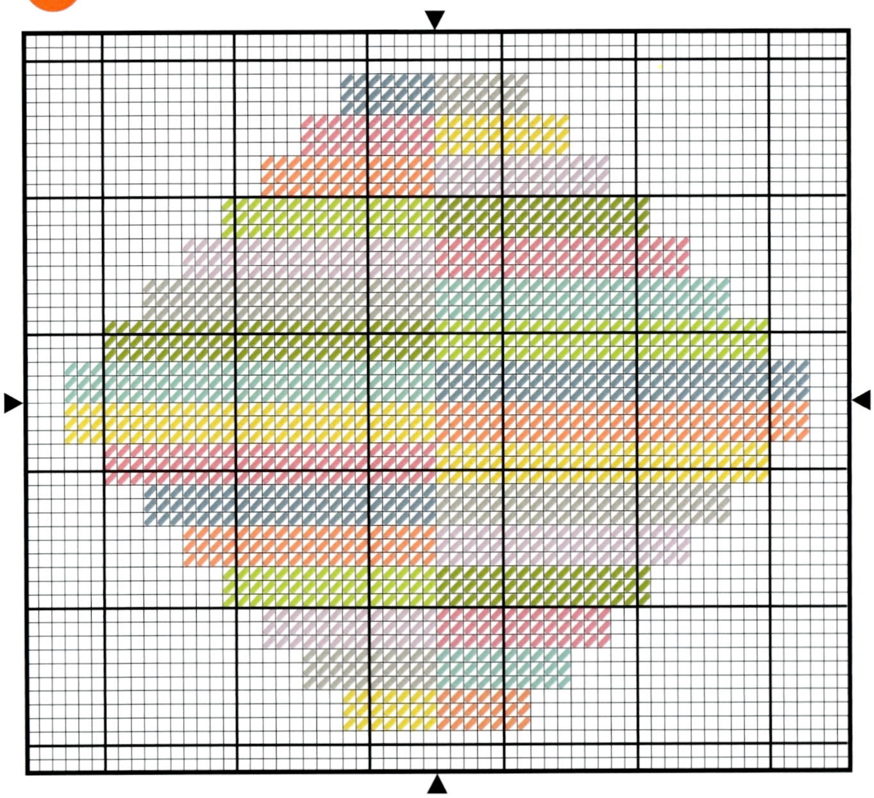

2

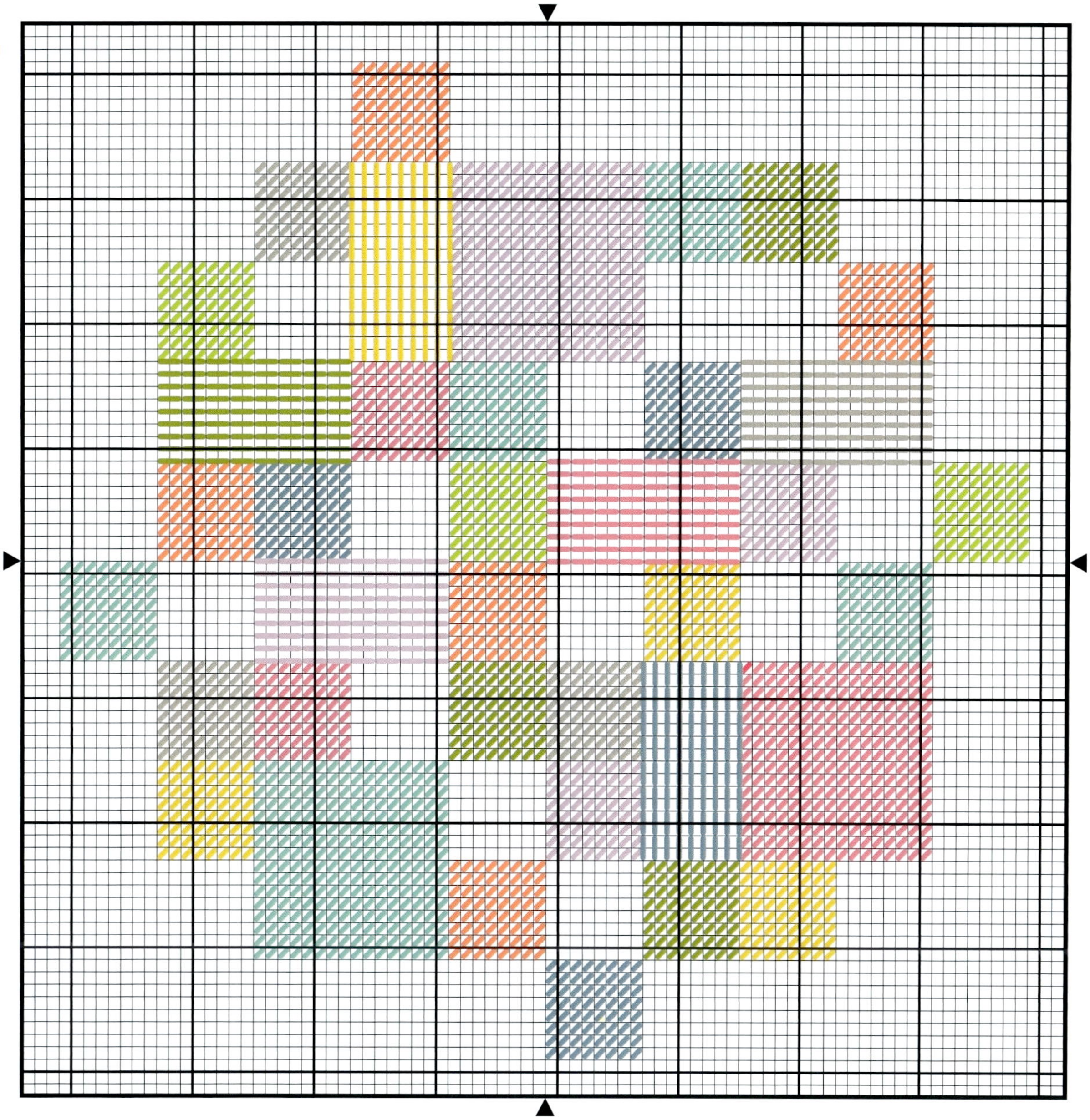

DMC Colors For Charts

X	DMC
	728
	3706
	3853
	210
	597
	3347
	472
	415
	993

3

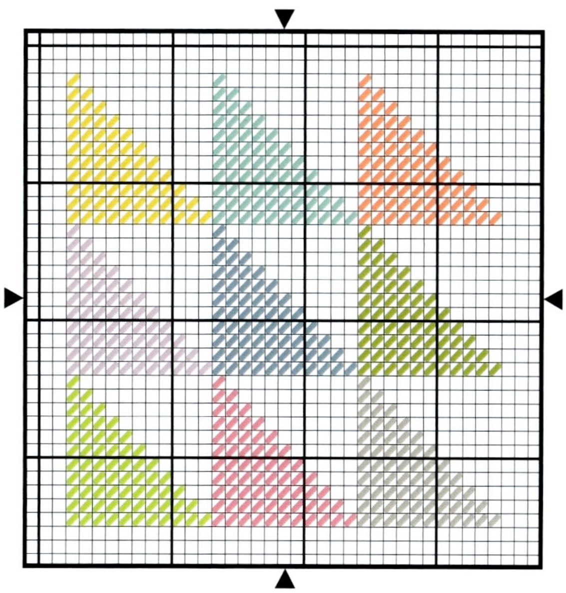

MCM TEA TOWEL SET

Finished Size: 2¼" x 13¼" stitched on a 15" wide x 25" long tea towel

STITCH GUIDE

- All Cross Stitches stitched over two fabric threads using 2 strands of floss.

SQUARE

44 squares x 44 squares

RECTANGLE

44 squares x 110 squares

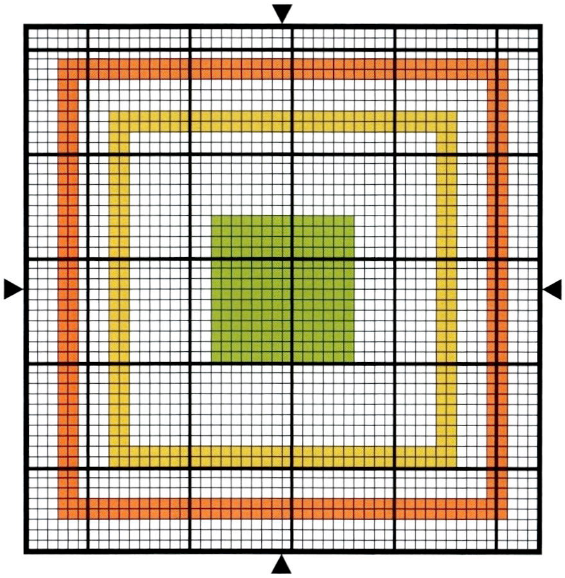

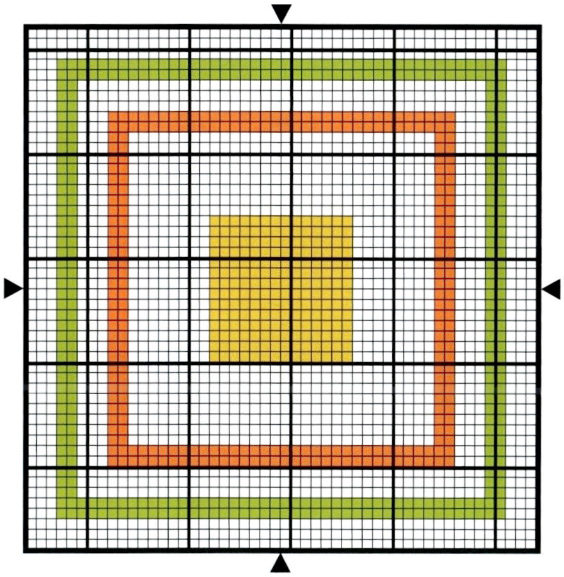

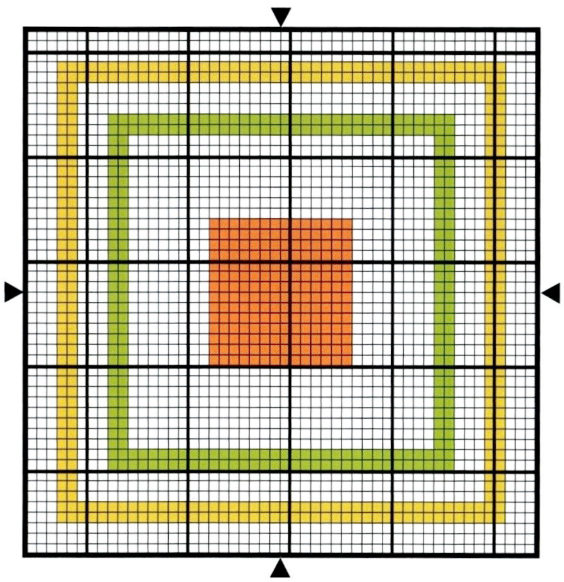

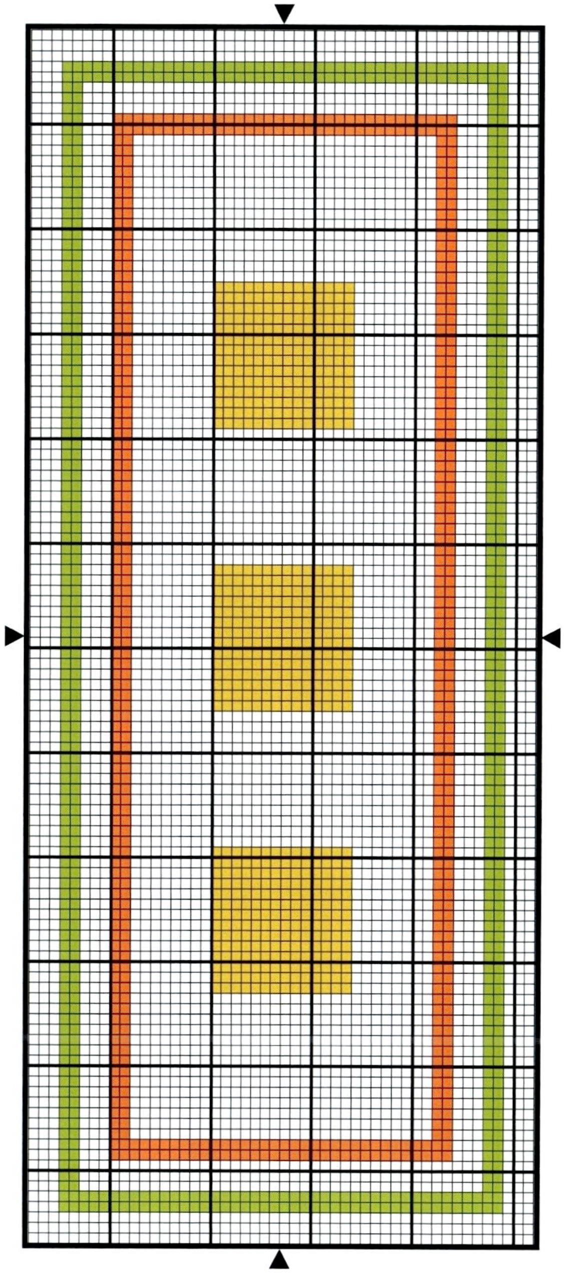

DMC Colors For Charts

X	DMC
(orange)	721
(yellow)	3852
(green)	470

RETRO PILLOW DUO

Finished Size:

Square pillow: 10½" x 10½" stitched on a 16" x 16" pillow cover

Lumbar pillow: 15⅞" x 10⅛" stitched on a 20" x 12" pillow cover

STITCH GUIDE

- All Backstitch stitched over two fabric threads using 6 strands of floss.

SQUARE PILLOW

104 squares x 104 squares

LUMBAR PILLOW

(ON NEXT PAGE)

158 squares x 101 squares

DMC Colors For Charts

X	DMC
	Ecru
	166
	992
	414
	Gray area indicates last two rows of previous section

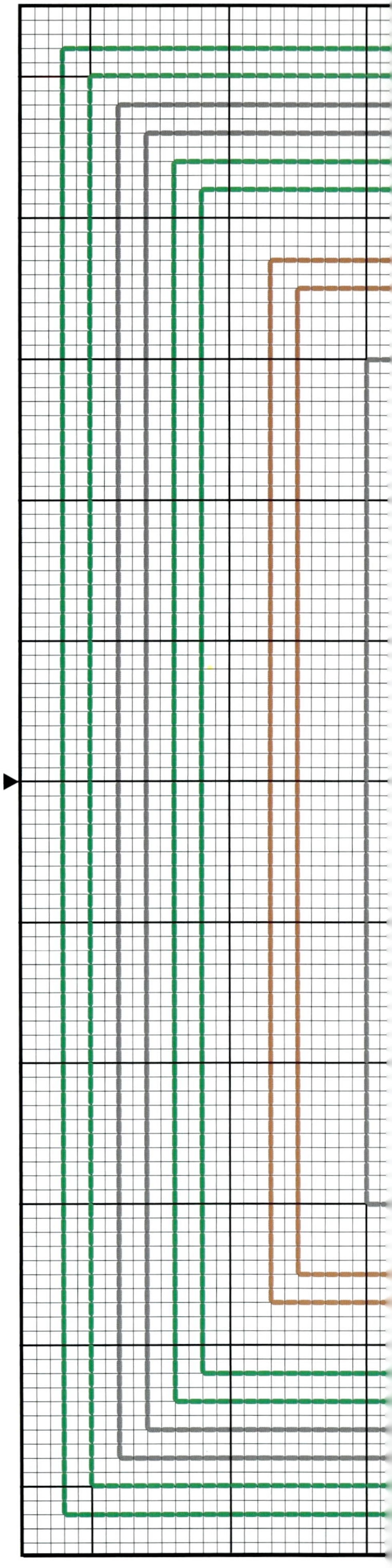

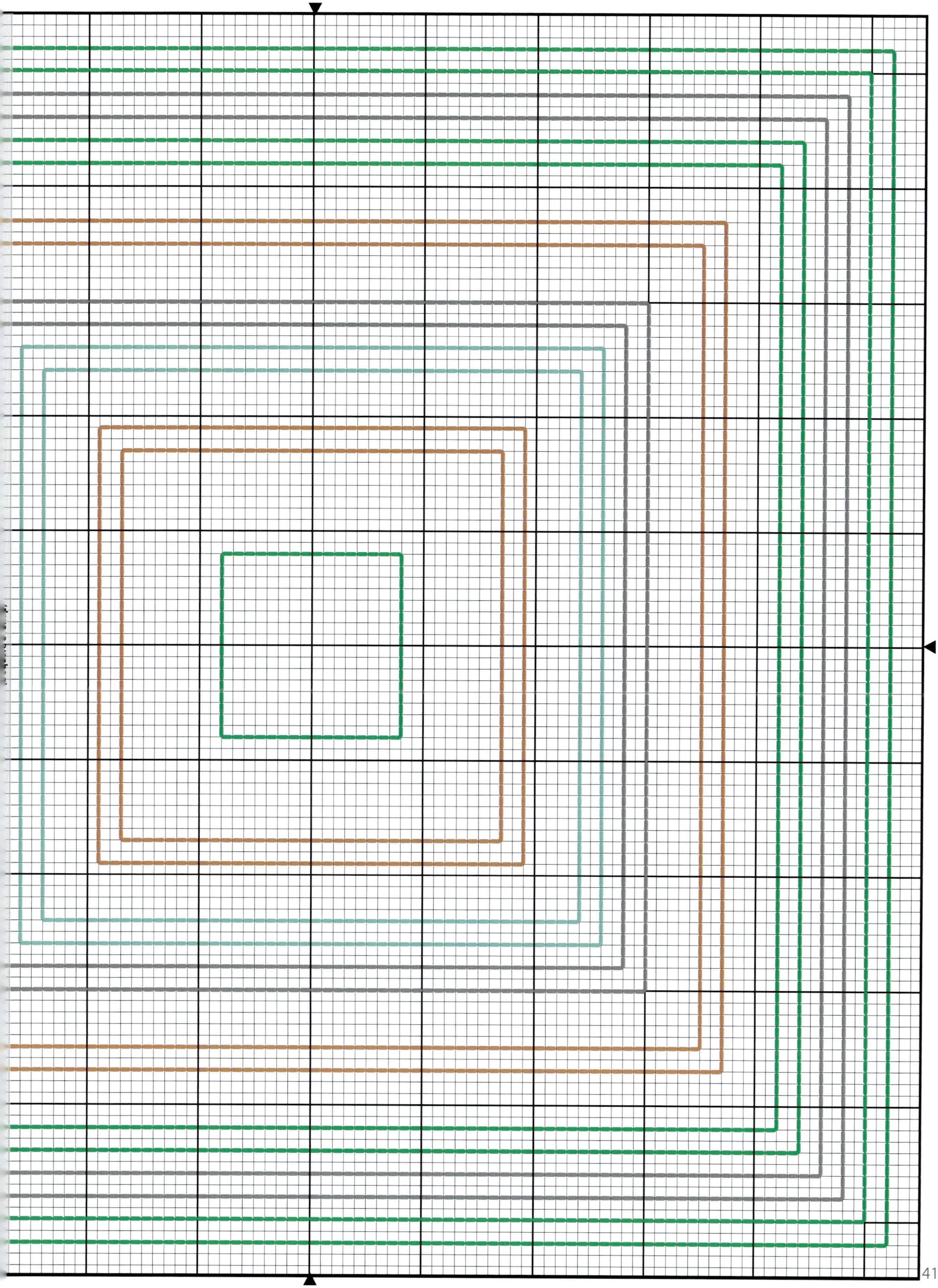

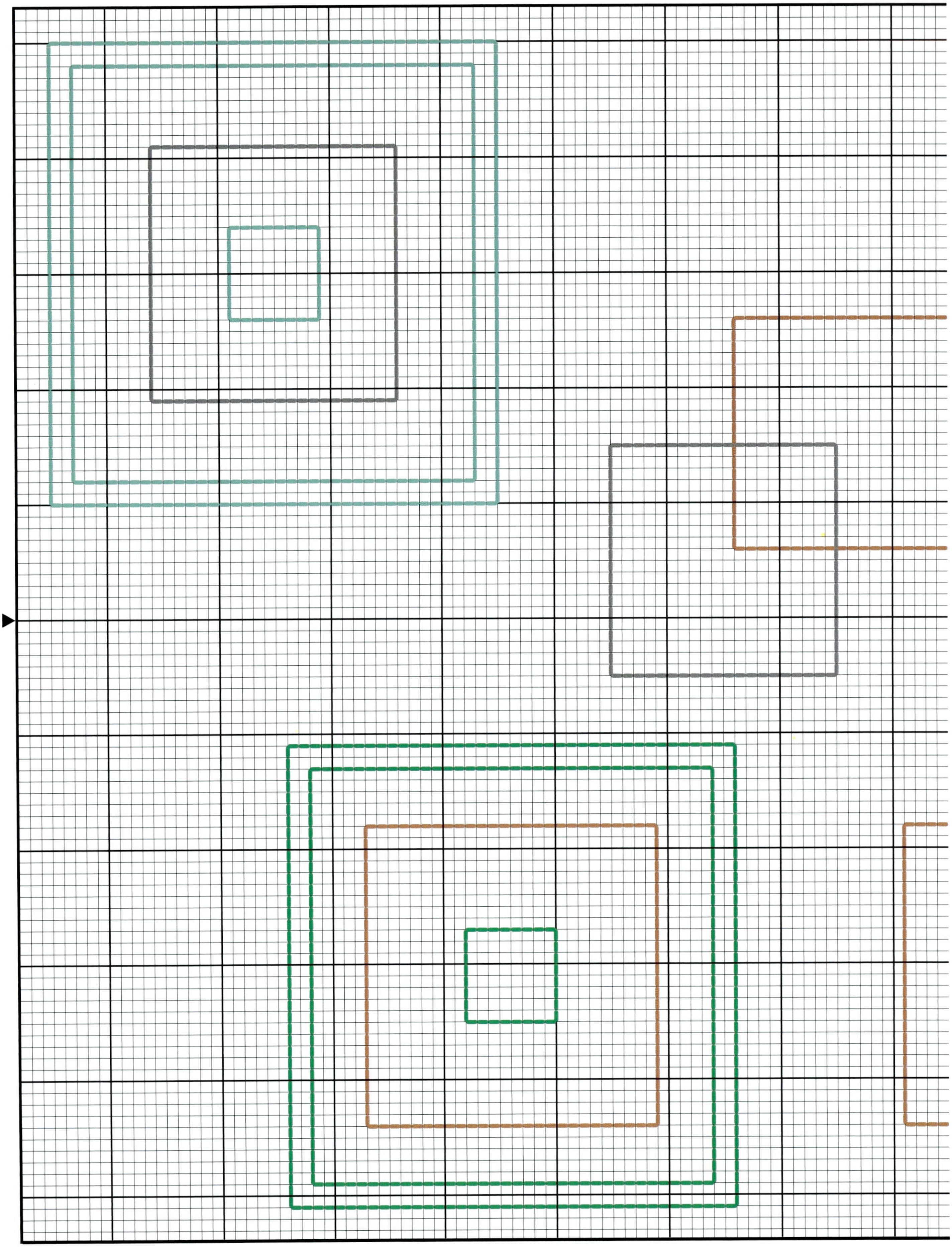

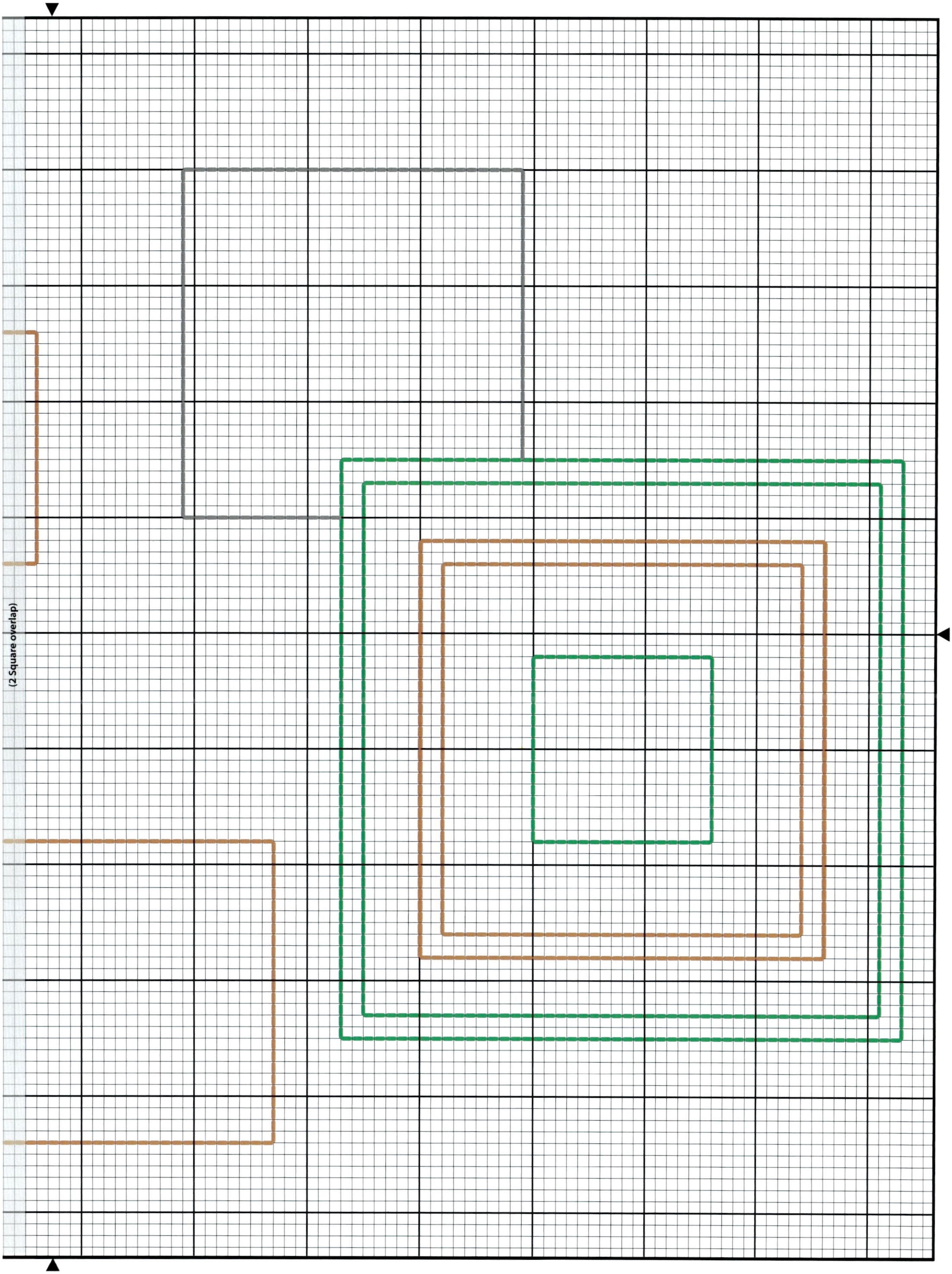
(2 Square overlap)

GENERAL INSTRUCTIONS

FABRICS

Aida Cloth

Aida cloth is an open, evenly woven fabric commonly used for cross stitching. This fabric has a natural grid forming the threads and leaving holes for the stitches. It is typically available in 10, 14 and 18 count. So, for example, a 10 count cloth will have 10 squares per inch. The natural stiffness of the Aida fabric allows you to work without an embroidery hoop on very small projects. For most projects, however, use an embroidery hoop to keep the work area tight and flat during stitching.

Aida is widely available in a few standard colors including white, natural and black. Occasionally you may find pastels, grays, burlap-look and holiday specific colors. It is not advisable to wash Aida prior to stitching as it may shrink and eliminate the desired stiffness. The finished project should be gently hand washed in cold water and only wash if necessary for cleaning off pencil or marker lines.

Aida cloth tends to fray at the edges. It is best suited for projects where the edges will be hidden in a hoop or photo frame for display.

TOOLS

Needles

A tapestry needle is used for Cross Stitch. Tapestry needles have a blunt point and a large oval-shaped eye. They work best with fabrics with distinct larger holes such as aida or evenweave fabrics or rigid materials such as plastic canvas and predrilled wood.

Choose a needle with an eye large enough to accommodate the floss thickness and that can also be pushed through the fabric you are stitching without enlarging the holes. The needle sizes indicated with each project supply list are recommendations. Most importantly, use a needle that you are comfortable with and can easily thread with the floss.

Needle Threader

A needle threader saves a tremendous amount of time. There are multiple brands available. I recommend the type made of solid metal with a hook or hole on the tip. Avoid the type with a wire loop made for regular sewing thread. The wire loops easily break especially when pulling thick or multiple strands of floss through a needle eye.

Marking Pencils and Water-Soluble Pens

Counted cross stitch is typically done by counting stitches and plotting your stitches area by area. Although not traditional, I find it very helpful to mark areas on my project to either outline a shape or designate where a color change will take place. I have spent too much time ripping out perfectly good stitches because I miscounted or stitched too far past where I was supposed to stop. For a light fabric, use a blue water-soluble pen. For a dark fabric, use a white or yellow fabric marking pencil. After completing your stitching, hold the project under running tap water. The pen and pencil markings will disappear in seconds. Place the piece right side down on a thick white towel. Press the piece dry from the wrong side with an iron temperature suitable for the type of fabric used. There are also "disappearing" markers for fabric but I don't recommend these as they take an unreliable time period to disappear.

Embroidery Scissors

Embroidery scissors are very helpful for all needlework projects compared to using regular sewing scissors. They are very small with curved blades. They allow you to snip off the floss very close to the knots and fabric surface. I used Westcott® Titanium Bonded 4" Curved Embroidery Scissors. There are other manufacturers making the same size scissors and they may work equally well.

Hoops

I prefer wooden hoops because they are very light. Some crafters like plastic hoops because they hold the fabric really tight. However this is entirely personal preference and I think you should use what you like.

It is best to choose a hoop that fits comfortably in one hand, while you stitch with the other. The hoop does not have to fully frame the embroidery pattern, it can be larger or smaller. I recommend removing the hoop from the project when it is not being worked on in order to avoid creasing the fabric with the hoop.

Magnifier

I never used a magnifier when I was younger. But if you are like me and now wear reading glasses, a magnifier is very useful to see the details more

"I absolutely love needle arts! I look forward to starting each day with a couple of hours of stitching. It is so relaxing and satisfying to see my designs come to life in this medium."

— DEBRA VALENCIA

clearly. I find that my needlework is neater and I can stitch a lot faster with a magnifier. There are different types on the market. I really like the Carson® LumiCraft™ "Hands-Free" LED Lighted 2x Power Magnifier with 4x Power Spot Lens. The adjustable cord allows me to hang it around my neck and it has a light that illuminates. It really helps to see the fabric weave better. It is not only hands-free but it moves along with your body as opposed to a tabletop model. For very close up work, I use a Fancii LED Illuminated Head Magnifier with interchangeable lenses. It fits over top of my reading glasses and has up to 3.5x magnification plus a built-in light.

Floss

Most floss colors are based on DMC® 6-strand embroidery floss, which is widely available. A few projects specify Pearl Cotton (Perle Coton) which is a thicker single strand floss. Each project chart has a color key identifying the colors used in these projects. Substitute similar colors as needed or feel free to change the color schemes to your own liking. You may also substitute your favorite brand of embroidery floss if you have a preference.

HOW TO READ CHARTS

Each chart is made up of a key and a color-coded chart on which each square represents a stitch. The number of stitches per inch varies from project to project and depends on materials used. Follow the charts provided in this book to obtain the same results. The chart is marked with arrows at the edge of the chart to identify the center of the design and with a heavier line every 10 stitches to aid in keeping your count. The colors in the key tell which DMC® or Eleganza™ floss or pearl cotton color to use for each stitch in the chart.

HOW TO STITCH

The horizontal and vertical centers of the charts are shown by arrows. To be sure the design will be centered, locate the center of the fabric by folding the fabric in half, side to side, and again top to bottom; mark this point with a straight pin. On the chart, count the number of squares from the center to where you wish to start. Then find your starting point by counting out the same number of fabric threads on the fabric. (To work over two fabric threads, count out twice the number of fabric threads.) For best results, it is best to start your stitches in the center of the fabric. Then work outward in each direction little by little.

When stitching, bring the threaded needle up at 1 and all odd numbers and down at 2 and all even numbers.

Cross Stitch: Over One

Cross Stitch is simply a classic "X" shape stitched in a grid. The results look best when the stitches are all going in the same direction. For example, you may notice that all stitches start at the bottom left, angling up to top right of the grid. The overlapping stitch always starts at the bottom right, crosses over the first stitch, angling up to the top left. The stitches can be worked horizontally or vertically **(Fig. 1)**. The number of stitches per inch varies from project to project and depends on materials used. Follow the charts provided in this book to obtain the same results.

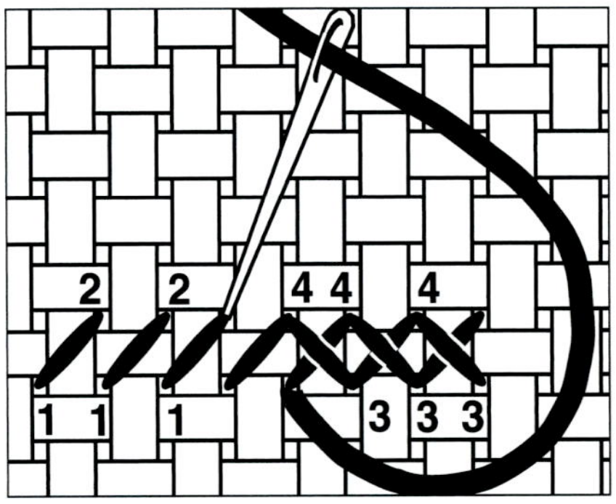

Fig. 1

Cross Stitch: Over Two

In many of my projects, I chose to use what is called "Over Two" Cross Stitch. This means you will use two squares or threads for one stitch **(Fig. 2)**. This will result in larger stitches which look especially good on larger projects. It will also reduce the number of stitches you have to stitch by 50%!

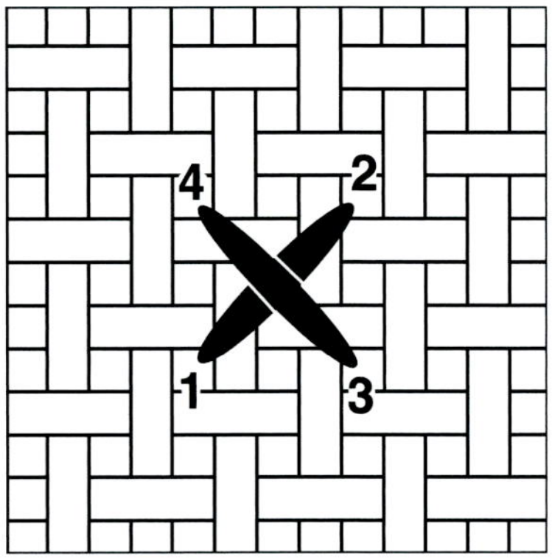

Fig. 2

For example, if you are working with Aida 14 count cloth and stitching over two, you will make 7 stitches per inch. You will stitch over two vertical squares or threads and two horizontal squares or threads to make one individual "X" shaped Cross Stitch.

Half Cross Stitch

A Half Cross Stitch is exactly as it sounds in that you will only stitch one diagonal stitch, then proceed to the next half stitch.

The results look best when the stitches are all going in the same direction starting at the bottom left angling up to top right of the grid **(Fig. 3)**.

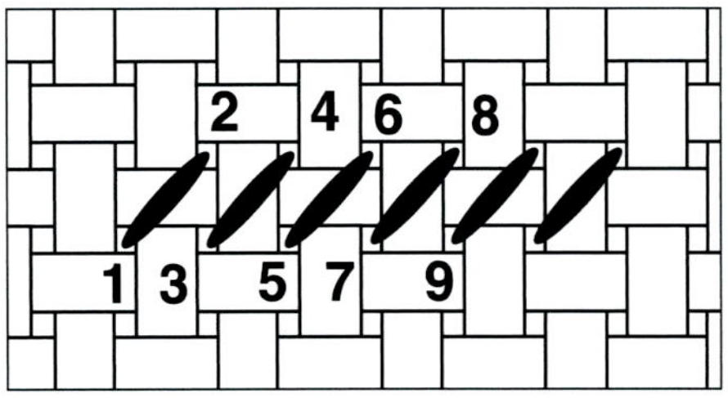

Fig. 3

Backstitch
The Backstitch is very useful for creating a single flat line of stitching (**Figs. 4a & 4b**).

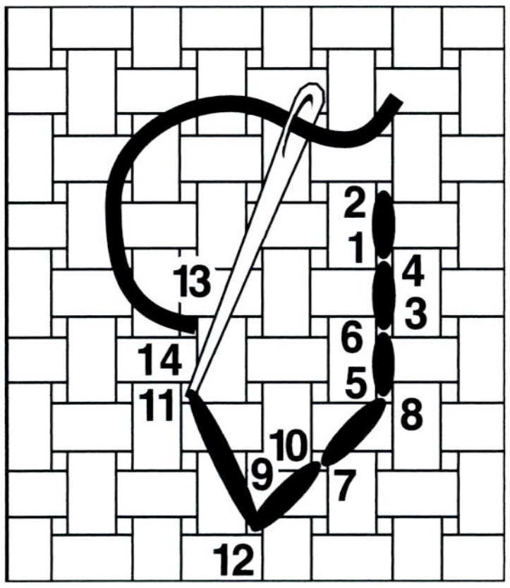

Fig. 4a

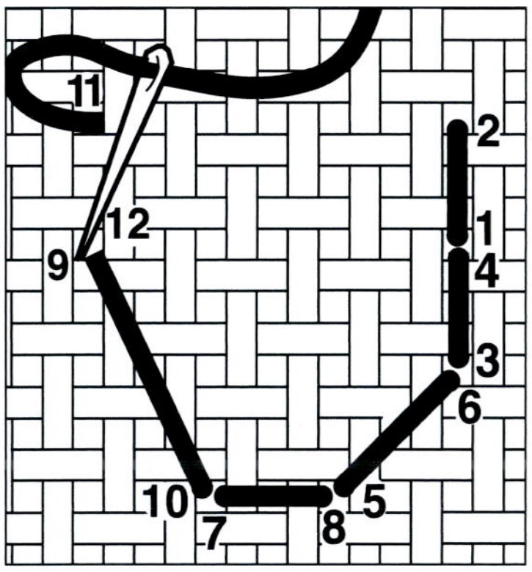

Fig. 4b

Blanket Stitch
The Blanket Stitch is very useful as an edging stitch to seam together two layers of fabric or simply finish any exposed edge (**Fig. 5**).

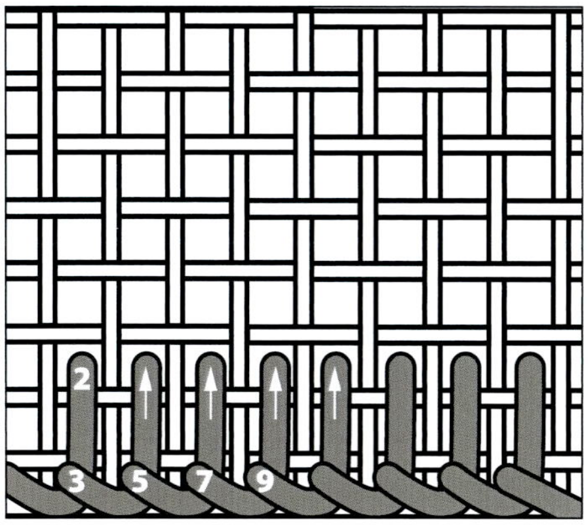

Fig. 5

Tips for Success

- Count stitches carefully, double checking the chart to the stitched piece frequently.
- For neat, consistent stitches:
  - Avoid splitting the floss with the needle when making each stitch.
  - Avoid piercing the cloth and instead push the needle clearly through the holes.
  - Keep consistent tension for all stitches.

USING HOOPS FOR DISPLAY

Embroidery hoops are a must-have tool for most stitching projects. They are also popular for framing a finished needlework. Try framing your next embroidery piece in a simple wooden hoop. The hoop framing method works well, and is also easy and inexpensive.

FINISHING THE HOOP BACK

Adding a fabric back is especially good for when you are making a hoop for a gift, as it looks more finished and professional.

Here are three options for finishing the back of your needlework:

Glue Gun
Using a glue gun is the fastest way to finish your hoop. Position your project in the hoop with the tightening screw perfectly centered at top. Turn your hoop face down on a clean surface.

Fig. 6

Trim the excess fabric off with scissors, leaving about 1" of excess fabric. Add a thin line of glue about 2" long to the inside rim of the hoop (**Fig. 6**). Press the fabric against the hoop until it sticks tightly to the surface. Add another line of glue to the next 2" or 3" and press fabric to hoop. Continue section by section until the entire selvage is glued to the hoop (**Fig. 7**).

Fig. 7

Gathered Back
If you do not have a glue gun, or simply prefer this method, it only requires a sewing needle and thread. Position your project in the hoop with the tightening screw perfectly centered at top. Turn your hoop face down on a clean surface.
Trim the fabric off with scissors, leaving about 1" of excess fabric (**Fig. 8**).

Fig. 8

With a simple long running stitch, also called basting stitch, sew around the entire back circumference of hoop. The stitches should be about ¼" from the inside edge of the hoop.

When finished sewing all around, pull the thread to tightly gather the fabric (**Fig. 9**). Make a Backstitch or two to hold the thread tight, then tie a knot, and trim off excess thread.

Fig. 9

Fabric-Covered Back

Using the inside hoop as a template, trace a circle onto a piece of quilters cotton or other matching fabric with a disappearing marker. Trim fabric about ½" outside the drawn line (**Fig. 10**). Using a warm iron, press the raw edge ½" to the back with wrong sides together.

Fig. 10

The fabric can be folded easily along a curve. Now, follow the steps for the "Gathered Back" detailed above. Then, with hoop facing down on a clean surface, pin the fabric-backing piece, right side up, onto back of hoop (**Fig. 11**). With a long running stitch, sew the fabric-backing piece to the gathered back. Continue all the way around the hoop and then secure the end with a hidden knot (**Fig. 12**).

Fig. 11

Fig. 12

Using a warm iron, press the raw edge ½" to the back with wrong sides together. For hanging the the hoop, simply add a short loop of ribbon, lace or matching fabric through the tightening screw.

Now your embroidery is ready for displaying, gifting or even selling!

Production Team: Publications Manager - Megan Copeland: Technical Editor – Lisa Lancaster; Graphic Designer – Michael Puckett; Photo Stylist – Lori Wenger; and Photographer – Jason Masters.

Made in U.S.A.